Dear Parents/Caregivers:

Children learn to read in stages, and all children develop reading skills at different ages. **Fisher-Price® Ready Reader Storybooks**™ were created to encourage children's interest in reading and to increase their reading skills. The stories in this series were written to specific grade levels to serve the needs of children from preschool through third grade. Of course, every child is different, so we hope that you will allow your child to explore the stories at his or her own pace.

Book 1 and Book 2: Most Appropriate For Preschoolers

Book 3 and Book 4: Most Appropriate For Kindergartners

Book 5 and Book 6: Most Appropriate For First Graders

Book 7 and Book 8: Most Appropriate For Second Graders

Book 9 and Book 10: Most Appropriate For Third Graders

All of the stories in this series are fun, easy-to-follow tales that have engaging full-color artwork. Children can move from Books 1 and 2, which have the simplest vocabulary and concepts, to each progressive level to expand their reading skills. With the **Fisher-Price® Ready Reader Storybooks**™, reading will become an exciting adventure for your child. Soon your child will not only be ready to read, but will be eager to do so.

Educational Consultants: Mary McLean-Hely, M.A. in Education: Design and Evaluation of Educational Programs, Stanford University; Wendy Gelsanliter, M.S. in Early Childhood Education, Bank Street College of Education; Nancy A. Dearborn, B.S. in Education, University of Wisconsin-Whitewater

Ready Reader Storybook™

Look at Lisa Go

Book 4

Written by C. Louise March • Illustrated by Gemma Page

Modern Publishing
A Division of Unisystems, Inc.
New York, New York 10022

Lisa likes to ride her bike on a bright day.

8

Lisa rides to the park where
she likes to play.

Lisa likes to skate.
She goes to the park rink.

Her skates have new laces.
They are bright pink.

Lisa rides a scooter.
She goes to her friend's pool.

Nick waves hello. He says,
"You look cool."

Lisa's friend Tess says,
"Drive my toy car."

19

"Look at me," Lisa says.
"I can go far."

Lisa gets a skateboard from her mom and dad.

22

24

When she rides on it,
Lisa is glad.

26

Lisa likes to move real fast.
Walking is too slow.

All of Lisa's friends say,
"Look at Lisa go!"

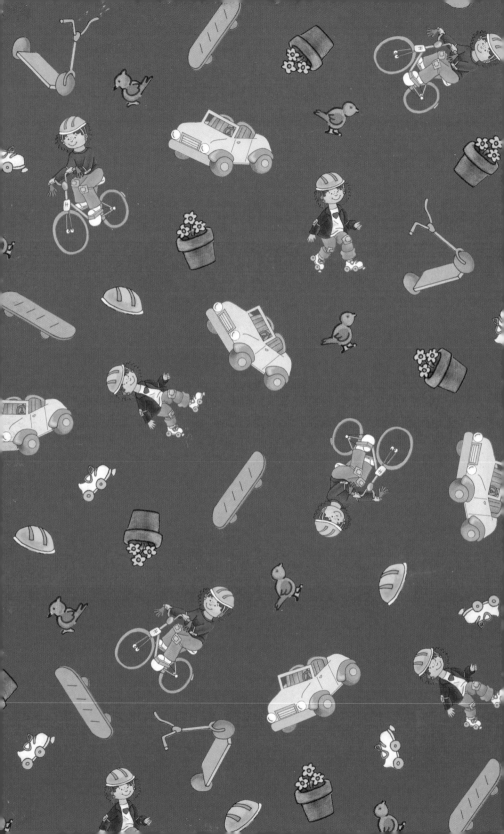